Ponytail

h

A division of Hodder Headline Limited

© Hodder Children's Books 2005
Published in Great Britain in 2005
by Hodder Children's Books
Text © Janet Rising
Illustrations © Jennifer Graham
Design by Andrew Summers
Cover design: Hodder Children's Books

The right of Janet Rising to be identified as the author of the work
has been asserted by him in accordance with the Copyright, Designs
and Patents Act 1988.

10 9 8 7 6 5 4 3 2

A catalogue record for this book is available from the British Library

ISBN: 0 340 90305 8

Printed by Bookmarque Ltd, Croydon, Surrey

The paper and board used in this paperback by Hodder Children's
Books are natural recyclable products made from wood grown in
sustainable forests. The manufacturing
processes conform to the environmental regulations of the country
of origin.

Hodder Children's Books
a division of Hodder Headline Limited
338 Euston Road
London NW1 3BH

Ponytalk

50 Ways To Make Friends With Your Pony

Janet Rising

h

A division of Hodder Headline Limited

Your pony will need time to settle in his new home. He has new friends to make, and has to get over those he has left behind. Resist the urge to ride and be with your new pony too much for the first few days, so he can adjust to his new surroundings.

If you are welcoming a new pony into your life, and she hasn't already got a name, find a name that really suits her. You may have dreamed of owning a pony called Silver, but that won't suit a bay cob at all. A name may pop into your head right away, or it could take a few days to assess your pony's personality. So, tempting though it may be, try not to rush into it!

Watch your pony in his stable. If he spends his time eating, drinking and snoozing, he is probably pretty happy. If he walks about, digs up his bed or fidgets as he looks over the door, he is obviously miserable and you can then take steps to help him. Turn him out in the field more - or all the time. Give him something to do or look at in his stable. You can get special shatterproof mirrors to fix to the wall, which will make him think he has company. Make sure he is getting enough forage to eat. You want him to feel at home!

Customise your pony's stable. A nameplate makes sure everyone knows it's her place - and no one else's. You can make one yourself by painting your pony's name on a piece of wood. Decorate it with painted horseshoes, or even a personal portrait of your pony!

If you don't want your pony to bump into things in the dark, don't trim his eyelashes or whiskers. These act as feelers and tell him where walls and the manger are in his stable, and where tree branches are in his field. They help him to find his food, too.

Create your pony's unique journal. Take time to discover what your new pony enjoys (ask his former owner, too). Write these down in a notebook so you don't forget them, and add any you discover for yourself. Draw an outline of either side of your pony and jot down every marking, scar and hair whorl on his body. Over time, include all your pony's achievements, his likes and dislikes, and when he is due to be wormed, shod and vaccinated. It will turn into your pony's very own life story!

Be your pony's masseuse! Find out where your pony likes to be massaged by using firm but gentle strokes all over her body. Watch her eyes and bottom lip; if she likes what you are doing, her eyes will close and her lower lip will drop. Ponies usually love having their eyes rubbed and their ears pulled very gently. Stroke her neck, and under her tail - stand to one side when you do this! It's a great way to get your pony to relax and bond with you.

Although your pony may worry you for treats which you enjoy eating, chocolate and sandwiches are not good for him. Share an apple or a carrot, instead! Remember to slice carrots lengthways as small discs can lodge in his throat and cause him to choke.

Next time you see your pony staring into the distance, try to discover what she is looking at. You may be surprised at how far she can see - a dog in the field, a tractor on the horizon, a model aeroplane. Horses and ponies have amazing distance vision, to help them survive in the wild.

Take time out for a pony watch. On a warm day, sit outside his field and note what your pony does, whom he hangs out with, when he eats and drinks and when he rests. This will give you an insight into his position in the herd and this can have a positive effect on your relationship, too. Low-ranking ponies let other ponies eat and drink before them. They are more likely to accept you as a herd leader. If your pony is the one who eats and drinks first, he is more likely to challenge everything you ask him to do, and you will need to be one step ahead of him to be in charge!

If your pony can't go out in the field for any reason, lead her to some tasty grass and let her graze in-hand. She'll love you for it! Make sure the grass is good to eat - grass verges next to busy roads are not the best places because the petrol fumes from cars can taint the grass. You want nice, tasty, clean grass.

Think like a horse! Ponies love company (that's why they live in herds), so it's no wonder your pony likes to hang out with his friends. Don't try to teach him anything when his friends are leaving the arena, or when they are all going out in the field and he has to stay behind. It would be better to pick a time when he is relaxed and more likely to give you his full attention.

Take a good, long look at your pony and decide which hairstyle would suit her best. Stocky cobs look fabulous with hogged manes and short tails. Graceful, lighter breeds look very glamorous with long, flowing manes and tails. Those in-between can look good with medium-length manes and tails. Whatever style you decide, it needs to suit your pony's shape and her personality - as well as your own.

Invite your pony along when you
and your friends get together. Ponies
love being included when you sit
down for a chat in the yard. And, if
you share your apples with them
they'll be happier still!

Don't get cross with your pony when she poos on the nice, clean bed you've just put down for her. She wants to make her stable smell of herself, so it really belongs to her.

Some ponies love to play with water. If your pony is a water baby, check his water bucket regularly - he may splash about so much, he'll have nothing left to drink! Take care when riding him through streams and big puddles as he may try to lie down and roll - with you still on him! A good warning sign is if he paws at the water with a front leg, so this is your cue to ride him on to dry land - quickly!

Be aware of your body language when you're with your pony. Avoid staring at her (her confidence will melt away), and don't square up to her with your hands on your hips (she'll get nervous). Instead, look slightly away from her and approach her sideways, keeping your hands low and speaking to her softly. This will give her lots of confidence.

If your pony opens his mouth too wide when he reaches for titbits, gently bump his nose with your closed fist. When he closes his mouth, quickly offer him the titbit again. This way, he will learn to take treats gently from your hand.

Ponies thrive on praise, just as we do. When your pony does something which pleases you, let her know! Give her a pat, or a titbit, or let her stop working. If you don't tell her, she won't know, and she won't try so hard for you next time!

Because of the way their eyes are situated on the sides of their heads, ponies cannot see directly under their muzzles, or directly behind their hindquarters. It is safer to approach your pony towards his shoulder so he has a clear view of you, and you avoid startling him. Never approach him from behind!

Watch your pony eating her feed. If she gobbles it down at speed whilst holding a front leg in the air, she may be scared someone is going to take her feed away. Ensure she is always left in peace and quiet when she eats, so she feels safe and secure.

Your pony can learn quite a lot of words - but it is how you say them that gives him an idea of what you want. For example, if you want your pony to slow down, use a tone which gets slower and softer as you say it. If you want to go faster, using a brisk, upward tone will give him the idea.

Make your commands very clear. Saying "Ter-rrrrrrot!" is better than a boring "Trot". Make sure every word is distinct - if you have two ponies called Harry and Barry, you could be in trouble. But if you make them different, saying "Har-eeee" and "Baaaaa-ry", for example, they will sound different to the ponies themselves.

Having trouble catching your pony in the field? As you get near to her, rustle some paper to get her attention. Then, walk slowly backwards. Her curiosity will get the better of her and she should walk towards you. Remember to reward her with a treat when you have her headcollar on.

To tell whether your pony is cold, feel his ears. They are a good indicator of his overall temperature. If his ears feel chilly, your pony is cold so put his rug on. If his ears are warm, he's fine!

During the summer, when the flies are bad, let your pony grow his forelock. If it hangs over his eyes, it will act as a fly curtain. Long tails can swish flies away, but watch out - if you are in the way, they can swish you too. Flying horsehair can really hurt!

Did you know that if you have a problem, your pony can help? Just explaining what is wrong can help to make things clearer in your own mind. You can whisper to her in her stable, or talk aloud to her when you ride. You may think that you've cleared your worry by talking about it, but your pony will know that she has transmitted her solution to you - and that you received it!

Ponies groom one another in the field by biting each other's withers. If your pony tries to nip you when you brush this area of his shoulder, remember this instinctive behaviour and try not to get cross with him. His instincts are getting the better of his good manners!

When you are riding, and your pony sees something which scares her, be her best friend. Give her a pat and tell her it's all right. Breathe regularly (if you hold your breath, she will be looking around to see what you are scared of!), and give her an example to follow. Let her take her lead from you; be a shining example!

Read your pony's mind. How? By looking at his ears! These tell you what he is thinking and where he is looking. Because each ear moves independently, your pony can listen to sounds coming from two different directions at the same time. When you are riding, watch for when your pony's ears hang either side of his head in a relaxed position. This means he is concentrating on you and what you are doing together. When his ears are like this, you have his attention.

If your pony is naughty, or behaving out of character, stop to think how you are feeling. If you've had a bad day at school, or are feeling upset about something, your mood could be affecting her. Take a deep breath and start again. You pony is trying to tell you something!

Be positive about your pony. Find
out what he's good at. He may be
the best pony in the world at being
caught, being led, or eating grass!
Discover his strengths and sing his
praises! The more you look for, the
more you will discover, and the more
you will be proud of him!

Watch your pony when she first goes out in the field on a cold day. She may gallop around with her mates with her tail in the air to get the tickle out of her toes. Then she will probably get down and roll in the muddiest place. This is to make her smell of the outdoors, rather than her stable, as this masks her smell from predators. Okay, so you know there are no wolves in her field, but her highly developed sense of survival doesn't allow her any time off!

Tie a turnip or a swede on a piece of string and hang it in his stable for your pony to munch on. Or roll one into his field and watch him chase it around. Ponies love to play with something they can eat, but if there is nothing else, you may see them playing with sticks they find in the field.

Did your pony jump out of her skin the last time you put your head over her stable door? Don't forget to speak to her to let her know you're there! She may be dozing, or engrossed in eating or playing with that swede you gave her. She'll be much calmer if she knows you'll always let her know when you're around.

Ponies usually give a warning when they get grumpy. Learn the signs; ears flat along the neck and a snaking head means "Watch out, I'm about to bite!" A swishing tail or a humped back means a kick is about to happen, so don't be around when it does!

Just like us, some ponies are very ticklish. If your pony suffers from being oversensitive when you groom him, use your hands to get off any dirt and mud in the ticklish places. He'll appreciate it.

Make your pony her own rosette.
Cut out a cardboard disk, stick her
picture on it, and sew pleated ribbon
around the edge. Sew on some tails
and there you have it - a decoration
for her stable.

Everyone wants to be a horse whisperer, someone who can tell what horses are thinking. Horse whisperers spend time observing horses to learn from them. Be a trainee horse whisperer by observing your pony and asking yourself why he does the things he does. Piecing the jigsaw together will enable you to learn what motivates your pony and his friends.

Think about how your pony views
the world. She can see in front of
her, either side of her and quite a
lot behind her, too. Next time she
seems nervous and jumpy,
remember that she may have seen
something you cannot.

Teach your pony his name. Call it in a distinctive way, maybe in a sing-song voice, and every time he responds, give him a treat. Soon he'll be galloping over to join you in the field when you call him!

There is nothing cosier than reading your pony a story. Of course, she won't understand the words but she will appreciate the closeness of it all and know you are doing something just for her.

Ponies hate being shouted at - it doesn't really mean anything to them, as they don't shout at one another. If you want to get your pony's attention, try whispering instead. His hearing is good enough and you can have a private conversation without anyone else listening.

Hide treats for your pony to discover when you are not there. Poke carrots and apples in straw bedding so she has something to find during the night. This makes the long time alone more interesting for her.

If your pony stays lying down when you visit him, this is a great sign that he trusts you, and you can feel very privileged. Do be careful when he gets up, though, as ponies are big and heavy, and they need room to stretch out their front legs before getting to their feet. Make sure you're not in the way!

Make Christmas decorations for your
pony. Thread carrots and apples -
even Polo mints - onto some string,
and tie it on the outside of your
pony's stable door. She'll have great
fun munching her festive garland!

On a cold day, add some warm water to your pony's water bucket. He will really appreciate it, and may drink more. You probably enjoy a warm drink in the middle of winter, rather than being faced with an ice-cold one. You don't want your pony to be thirsty, just because the weather is cold.

If you have long hair, share hairstyles with your pony! Put in plaits or bunches and tie with coloured ribbons. Take a photograph and send it to your grandparents and see whether they can spot who's who!

Ponies cannot see immediately under their noses so don't be surprised if yours nips your fingers when you offer her a treat! Always offer treats on the flat of your palm, with your thumb tucked in, so there are no misunderstandings. Your pony will be as disappointed as you when she finds out what she thought was a carrot is really your finger!

When you pull your pony's mane, or if your pony loses tail hairs, save them to make a bracelet for you to wear. Plait the hair and fasten the ends together. Then, you will always have a reminder of your wonderful pony, wherever you go.